ALSO BY JONATHAN GALASSI

POETRY

Morning Run
North Street
Left-handed

NOVELS

Muse
School Days

TRANSLATIONS

The Second Life of Art: Selected Essays of Eugenio Montale
Otherwise: Last and First Poems of Eugenio Montale
Eugenio Montale: Collected Poems, 1920–1954
Eugenio Montale: Selected Poems
Giacomo Leopardi: Canti
The Poetry of Primo Levi

The Vineyard

*

THE VINEYARD

*

Jonathan Galassi

ALFRED A. KNOPF
NEW YORK
2026

A BORZOI BOOK
FIRST HARDCOVER EDITION
PUBLISHED BY ALFRED A. KNOPF 2026

Copyright © 2026 by Jonathan Galassi

Penguin Random House values and supports copyright. Copyright fuels creativity, encourages diverse voices, promotes free speech, and creates a vibrant culture. Thank you for buying an authorized edition of this book and for complying with copyright laws by not reproducing, scanning, or distributing any part of it in any form without permission. You are supporting writers and allowing Penguin Random House to continue to publish books for every reader. Please note that no part of this book may be used or reproduced in any manner for the purpose of training artificial intelligence technologies or systems.

Published by Alfred A. Knopf, a division of Penguin Random House LLC, 1745 Broadway, New York, NY 10019.

Knopf, Borzoi Books, and the colophon are registered trademarks of Penguin Random House LLC.

Portions of this work were previously published in *The New Yorker* and *Poetry Nation*.

LIBRARY OF CONGRESS CATALOGING-IN-PUBLICATION DATA
Names: Galassi, Jonathan author
Title: The vineyard / Jonathan Galassi.
Other titles: Vineyard (Compilation)
Description: First hardcover edition. | New York : Alfred A. Knopf, 2026.
Identifiers: LCCN 2025021061 (print) | LCCN 2025021062 (ebook) | ISBN 9780593803790 (hardcover) | ISBN 9780593803806 (ebook)
Subjects: LCGFT: Poetry Classification: LCC PS3557.A387 V56 2026 (print) | LCC PS3557.A387 (ebook) | DDC 811/.54—dc23/eng/20250623
LC record available at https://lccn.loc.gov/2025021061
LC ebook record available at https://lccn.loc.gov/2025021062

penguinrandomhouse.com | aaknopf.com

Printed in the United States of America
1st Printing

The authorized representative in the EU for product safety and compliance is Penguin Random House Ireland, Morrison Chambers, 32 Nassau Street, Dublin D02 YH68, Ireland, https://eu-contact.penguin.ie.

For Tenoch

pretend peace,
peaceful almost as peace.

—GEORGE JOHNSTON

Contents

*

THE VINEYARD

3

ECLOGUE

83

ORIENT EPITHALAMION

89

The Vineyard

*

The Vineyard

A ripe peach is already cooked.

The vineyard was always better than the grapes.
We live beside one here in Oyster Ponds
and get to watch them grow all summer.
There's an arbor, too, behind the house—
two in fact—and a wisteria vine
between them, sprouting suckers
on the lawn, among the ferns,
rabid for conquest. But the local grapes,
Vitis riparia, Vitis labrusca,
Concord or Catawba, leave a lot to be desired.
"Every old farm on the east end of Long Island
has a grapevine on a trellis
between the backdoor and the outhouse,"
writes Louisa Thomas Hargrave in her memoir,
The Vineyard, in which she tells
how she and her then-husband, Alex, planted
the first vines on the North Fork of Long Island
in the early seventies. These native grapes
are why Leif Eriksson called the East Coast
Vinland; as the name implies,
they're distant cousins
of the European *vinifera* species
"good" wine is traditionally made from.
But the homegrown vines
"grow like tall, ungainly weeds," Louisa writes,
"trying to reach the tops of trees in the forest
to get a little sunlight on their big,
hairy"—botanists say "pubescent"—leaves.
They're known as "foxy" for their earthiness

and tang, and, she adds, it's "not a compliment."
I used to imagine the raccoons
going for them after Labor Day, once we were gone,
skins and twigs, downed leaves and scat
staining the cement floor behind the kitchen.
Or we'd dream of distilling
a really potent kerosene-like grappa
from the detritus. Fred loves, or used to love,
his grappa industrial-strength,
and what could be rougher on the tongue than this?

But the vineyard next door's different.
It aspires to an amateur's refinement,
with fifteen rows of five varietals
and stones and shells laid out beneath the rows
with grass paths in between—although no rose trees at the ends
the way there sometimes are in grown-up vineyards,
to attract the too-few bees.
This place was Dr. Held's delight, his Sabine farm.
We used to see him upright on his Segway
like a lictor in his chariot,
harrying the hapless deer—
not that he dissuaded them for long.
Nothing dissuades them. They show up
on the back lawn afternoons, nosing for early apples
that might have dropped from the old trees—
which don't give off much fruit these days
(last year, though, they were splendiferous,
their blossoms were like snowdrifts through the village).
The poor dears act offended that we're here
and barely deign to saunter out of sight
when I go to the trouble of pretending
to try and scare them.

They're not frightened in the least;
it's really too much work for them, or me,
to make a fuss, although I bark and wave my arms,
acting out my annoyance. Our landlord, Dave,
has put up fencing at the back of the yard
and set out some blue barrels behind the barn
to make it a bit harder—just a bit, though—
for them to reach the lawn;
but they come anyway—and who can blame them?
They're being hemmed out
like the Scots farmers by Enclosure:
there's nowhere left for them.
Evenings I watch them lope
along the steel fence of the tree farm
across the street, seeking a way in.
Not to worry. They'll be back.

Suzanne and Tom live on the other side,
beyond the enormous clumps of tiger grass
that remind me of the Japanese seaweed
whose name I can't remember, the one we eat
with sushi that gets stuck between my teeth.
Wakame, thank you. So many names
don't jump to mind these days:
"nominating difficulties," we say now,
hardening of the arteries, it once was.
Since we pruned the deadwood
out of the huge old arborvitaes
the vineyard's almost part of the back yard—
with just a meshwork fence between us and it.
But once the vines grow up and out
I can't see the road on the far side
unless a boat glides by up on its trailer.
Early last spring there was a dead branch

jutting out from the luscious yellow cedar
that stands among the grasses by the road.
The way it spoiled the view annoyed me,
so I drove over with my saw and lopped it off.
Tityrus, you saw me from the bathroom
and texted to compliment me on
my drive-by pruning.
But the tree looked so much shapelier,
so naturally symmetrical,
albeit with its sunlit southern side,
that I was satisfied all day
as if I'd righted a wrong.

Now we've learned that Dr. Held
died last winter. I had always hoped
to try his wine,
to sample what the land here tastes like—
not that I had great hopes for it;
truth be told, I don't exactly love
the North Fork's acid wines.
The water table here in Oyster Ponds
isn't that hospitable to grapes:
too wet, too saline: too close to the sea.
I imagined his as heavy, syrupy,
not jammy like a California Cab
or a steroidal Super Tuscan
but sharp—or else too sweet,
or sour, like him—or both,
not unlike the wine that our *baresi* neighbors
used to make in Carroll Gardens,
stomping the grapes down in their basement vat
to make what they drank all winter.
But Dr. Held was rather brusque
(I used to call him Dr. No)

and I never got around to asking him
to sell us a few bottles.
I almost wandered over there one day
but heard him shouting, so I put it off.
And now I've missed my chance;
so much for my adventure in *terroir*.
Was the cedar branch an omen?
What will happen to this piece of world?
Dan, who cares for vines on the North Fork,
told me the good doctor's family
wants to keep the vineyard,
in honor of their father's passion.
I hope so; but you have to wonder.
They're certainly not making wine
the way he did; how could they, living in L.A.?
Now the fruit—three rows each of merlot, cabernet,
Riesling, cabernet franc, cabernet sauvignon—
will be sold off to a dealer
who'll toss them into some varietal vat.
We'll never know the vineyard's wine,
savor what this place is really made of.
There's another one out the Main Road
on the way to the Point,
although the vines there grow in open fields
with unimpeded sun and wind.
These two little plots, in fact, are practically
the only North Fork vineyards this far east.
They're rich men's playthings. If I were rich
I'd want to live surrounded by my grapes,
watch them fatten and be harvested,
if they weren't consumed by fire,
while I led my desultory life.
And now I have the next best thing next door!
I love the way the vines have made this landscape,

how they've helped preserve the sense
of "Kansas on the Atlantic," as my friend
George put it: farms by the water,
a world that's almost been erased
by the South Fork's pleasure seekers—
and more and more out here, too, given that
we're only a hundred miles from Sin City.
As always, we're the problem;
we bring it with us, just like picnic litter.
George grew up
in the heart of South Fork beauty,
Sagaponack's fake simplicity:
old farmhouses then, McMansions now,
raked paddocks, vegetables arrayed like flowers.
William Merritt Chase's
scenes of shore life at Shinnecock
painted at his wide-porched "cottage" in the dunes
evoke a world of sun and sand and wind,
unruly crinolines, boaters, parasols.
His art school on Canoe Place Road
was stocked with children, dogs, and housemaids,
the oak-paneled studio laid
with carpets, satin drapery, and undressed models.
Chase was of the ilk of James and Sargent,
flamboyant in his pale suit on the sand.
This was before one actually swam.
Decency laws discouraged seaside nudity.
Ladies in black bathing costumes
sat in their four-wheeled "machines,"
mini-shacks that got rolled into the water,
where the waves washed decorously over them.
It was only at the turn of the last century
that the South Fork's ninety miles
of untouched Atlantic beach turned fashionable

and mustachioed hearties in striped onesies
conquered the surf.
When the railroad came out to East Hampton,
the cottages of Maidstone, Water Mill, and Quogue
sprang up overnight, and the North Fork
retired into agricultural abeyance.
Now mogul palaces
nestle beside the Trianons
of the old industrialists' heirs,
ha-has and circular drives,
instant lawns and ponds and trucked-in
fifty-foot trees,
deer splayed statuesquely in the orchards.
We're simpler here, where the old farmers'
and fishermen's snug houses
huddle by the harbor. Our scale
is more humane, we tell ourselves;
but we're squatters, too, invaders,
scarfing up the quiet
any way we can.

Well-named taciturn tall Alex Hargrave
sat beside me on the hard black chapel bench
at school and neither of us said a word.
It was only a few years afterwards that he and Louisa
began their foolhardy, revolutionary
venture on the Devil's Belt,
the rough-and-tumble tree-shorn back
of Long Island's beyond, rubble pushed up
out of the Sound by the Harbor Hill moraine
during the Wisconsin glaciation
nineteen thousand years ago.
Long Island was invaded from the sea
by sailors making forays down the coast

from Massachusetts and Connecticut,
which is why this sometimes feels like home.
The English feared attacks by the Armada
and felled the forests by the shore
so they could see them coming. Farewell, white oaks.
You have to go to Gardiner's Island out in Gardiner's Bay
or maybe Mashomack Preserve on Shelter Island
(home of the Mashomack Special!)
to find a first-growth
stand of the great trees that predominated here.
The same Gulf Stream
that keeps the Médoc temperate (or used to)
passes this way (or did); the climates
weren't so dissimilar, which was the vintners' luck.

In 1973, Louisa tells us,
Cutchogue "was a post office,
a dingy pharmacy, a 'variety' store
with inventory that hadn't been touched
since the 1930s"; but "what the Village
lacked in shopping, it made up for in churches."
Oyster Ponds two hundred years ago
was a farming and a shipping hub.
After visiting in 1804,
Timothy Dwight of Yale observed,
"The land is good, and the people
are industrious and thrifty . . .
The agriculture has lately been much improved,
but the people suffer not a little
from ecclesiastical contentions."
And so today: too many churches,
too few worshipers. By 1842 there were 500 souls
in need of nourishment in Oyster Ponds,
no longer just the founding families

(some of them still here today) but *incomers*,
they were called. Village Lane descended
from the highway to the dock in the deep harbor,
where the little yacht club sits,
and the street floods after heavy rain.
On Bosn's Lane, which hooks off to the west,
the rich shipowners
and the one whaling captain, Mr. Brown,
built their humbly ostentatious houses,
with wide porches and fake widow's walks.
Now the old boat in the yard next door
and the yard behind us,
where now and then a winch cranks
or a motor drones, are what's left to remind us
more than the faint salt breeze which dies at night
that this is still (or was)
a fisherman's more than a sailor's place.

Avaricious country life—so many motor sounds
I take the refrigerator's hum
for baseline quiet, and when it's truly still
I'm awed by the silence—
pure bird silence (if such a thing exists).
We don't hear it the way we sense
the rumbling, say, in Zankel Hall
when we watch Paul Lewis playing Schubert
(do you think he hears it?).
And there's the upper buzz of something else—
is it instinct or conscience,
when I put in my hearing aids
and suddenly hear the crickets?
We know the power's out when the generators
start coughing up and down the street,
if a drunk driver hits a phone pole

on the causeway or a storm blows in,
which is often enough. At night, though,
there's no wind. Nothing moves
except the deer browsing at their salad bar:
I tell myself I hear hooves on the asphalt
but in fact they're absolutely stealthy.
They only snort a little when they're scared.

There are five trees in front of me
as I sit at my desk this morning:
the mulberry, its spindly sticks still barren;
and just behind, a hemlock
(two in fact, combining into one,
yin and yang, the way trees sometimes do);
then the golden cedar,
the one whose branch I hacked,
and, in Suzanne's front yard,
a broad umbrella pine that sambas
in the vivid wind,
and a perfect common sugar maple—
my team, my consiglieri;
and the other timeworn, ragged maple
this side of the fence,
next to the eight forsythias
which Dave planted for our privacy,
eventually to be one hedge, with the butterfly bush
that horned in in between
and the spirea volunteering over the fence.
The late-blooming cherry-red crape myrtle
we planted nearer to the house
is still leaflorn. But now
the mulberry explodes into lime-green flame
and the little nubbly fruits
that silkworms love will darken soon and fall

sticky and stinky on the tarmac.
Then the crape myrtle will start sending out
the red needles where its bolls
of blossom will eventually grow.
Will these trees be able to live out
their natural two hundred years
the way I hope to live out mine?
Many of their kind will evanesce,
usurped by invaders from the south
as our climate turns less temperate.
I heard a geologist tell us this
on a pandemic Zoom one day,
matter-of-factly signing our death warrants.
Tish, the architect across the way
(I call her Tish, although we've never met),
is reshingling her house
with its perfectly pruned orchard,
each tree hung with absolutely spherical
green-going-to-red apples and a few
callipygian pears like ornaments
or those unreal gold-wrapped holiday specimens
from Harry & Dave.
The unmown meadow underneath the trees
used to be a monarch station
and maybe still is.
They were everywhere in August—
on the butterfly weed and butterfly bush
and the butterfly vine (although the one thing
monarch larvae eat is milkweed leaves),
and those ubiquitous white moths enlacing the borders.
They're fewer, though, each year,
lasting while the sun lasts
the way the hummingbird,
who's back again, you say,

from God knows where
with his mother-of-pearl tail feathers
stays till he's gone.

What's a weed but a plant in the wrong place?
There were huge Verbascum sentinels
growing out of the crevices in the vast
stone terraces at Chatsworth.
I'd thought they were mulleins,
those wild corncobs poking out
of their lamb's-ears trousers
everywhere along the road. But no, it turns out
they or their cultivated cousins
are cherished rarities with Latin names.
Our kind proliferate in the Haffenreffers' field,
where milkweed rules along with curly vetch,
cruel purple bindweed.
Their cutting garden was miraculous
behind its deer fence altar screen,
flanked by two huge heraldic stripes
of lavender and Russian sage.
From the little park by the secret beach
I like to steal a swim at with Suzanne
or build sandcastles with Luka
we could glimpse the hidden lily beds
behind their house, a yellow-orange bower
unshared with the likes of us,
or maybe anyone.
At their honesty cart out front
they sold bouquets in jam jars
and extra vegetables and plants
for the benefit of Greenways Hospital,

whose emergency room we know and love,
the one the famous Opportunity Shop
also supports
where Caitlin has been known to purchase shirts
and we pick up old trays and dishes,
hand-me-down finds, for a buck or two.
I love sipping whiskey of an evening
in the fifty-cent old cordial glasses
that sat unloved on someone's mother's shelf
until we came along. But I digress.

Here's what I can see from the kitchen window
(partial inventory): ancient mounded pink spirea,
unnamed crimson cottage rose,
oak-leaf and lace-cap hydrangea,
black-and-blue salvia, thistle, allium,
thalictrum (meadow rue to you) and phlox
—magenta, white, and lavender—
lavender, and creeping phlox,
cimicifuga, lamb's ears, cleome
(although they want more sun),
trumpet vine, *Verbena bonariensis*
(meaning that it hails from Argentina!),
ever-unsuccessful morning glory,
cosmos (they need full sun as well,
as do the dahlias and zinnias
and the clematis I'm hopeless with).
I love the homely, not the Latin names,
which shows you what an amateur I am,
but call a cane a cane.
And red maple in the neighbors' yard
that gradually turns green with crimson edges,
cranberry euonymus, everyday azalea,
scraggly yew, and unloved rhododendron.

The vitex, spiky emphatic purple glory,
gets its superb two weeks in July and August
(everything gets two weeks, like us,
plus two of anticipation
and one of grieving): and, yes, forsythia,
apple, wisteria, and bridal wreath,
iris, peony—the season's slow parade.

Last year Beau Harris and his crew of artists
cut the dead high branches out of the cedars,
(they're known as arborvitaes, too,
trees of life). They're primal, sculptural;
Beau called them dinosaurs.
When we first came they were conical,
their lower branches silver deadwood
down to the ground. We hacked the old dead branches back
and dragged them off behind the barn
and the Burtons carted them away.
Underneath were living branches
which we used as swings,
immense ideograms expressing unreadable things,
before they got vestigial and died, too.
Afterwards, the apple tree behind them looked rachitic.
The old thing still bore in the upper register,
but it was misshapen, leggy,
wormy, like me. Charles helped me prune it, though,
and it was happy for another year
before it went to its reward.
Charles, our tutelary garden god,
showed up with his saws and ladders
and the electric pruner that I bought
to thank him for his aid and inspiration.
Our Oyster Ponds Pomona, our Apollo/Dionysus,
tall, fine-profiled, garrulous,

big-footed, generous.
Who *is* the god of gardens?
(I looked it up now on my phone.)
Why, it's Priapus (I'm just saying)
with his reed basket and bludgeon
and ever-ready smile. We all try to *act as if,*
the way the Big Book says;
but Charles *knows*. He inherited his garden
from Freddie's brother Skip, an even more
let's say inclusive plantsman,
who never saw a specimen he didn't want
to fold into his three-eighths of an acre.
He named his garden Adsworthy; it sounds
ancestral-adjacent, but it's so-called because
he met Charles through a personal column
in a local paper (do these still exist?).
Adsworthy got so socked-in in Skip's day
that his cottage garden morphed into
an Amazonian leaf maze,
with overhanging boughs
arcing every which way.
There was no patch of simple sun
a plant could thrive in, which is why
it became a tropical shade garden
(the plants spent the winter months indoors,
which made things quite tight in their small house).
But Charles impresses me
with how he understands sun-loving plants
make do with what they get,
not unlike most folks I know
(doesn't each of us contend with shade
being thrown by somebody or something?).
In the decade since Skip died
Charles has made Adsworthy his.

It's still mystical, mysterious,
but shapelier, more open,
with lights and darks and colors
calling across its bigger, airier room.
It tells its story as you trace the paths
past fifty hosta species, epimediums, and lilies,
under Victor and Frances,
twin Silver Parasol magnolias, of which
there are only one or two examples
anywhere, if I don't err.
Skip and he adopted them as seedlings
from the Arnold Arboretum
and raised them like children,
till gradually they soaked up all the light,
the way that a new generation can.
Sinan, who is Charles's husband now,
has repainted their godmother Frances Leventritt's
weighty cast-iron Garden District furniture
which might have been props in *The Glass Menagerie*
but sat in fact on her Martha's Vineyard patio
before they found their afterlife at Adsworthy.
Skip had painted them a bold chartreuse
but now they're demure gunmetal gray
—elegant foils for the riot around them.
We sit and sip a ruby-red *Clairet*
and admire the roses that go on forever
(who *was* Mme. Isaac Péreire?).
And sometimes Charles, our faun of the eighth decade,
calls on our amateur demesne
and offers mild, encouraging suggestions,
scattering his benign regard
in his honeyed Appalachian accent
about our pedestrian (he doesn't say so) plantings,

then moves on through the village,
spreading stardust health and happiness.

All this productivity
in a place about peace
when the sun comes up at five
and the deer are still in the street
marauding the bushes.
Someone runs by at 5:10 every morning.
I stand in the shadows by the window
and wait to see him underneath the streetlamp
but either he's too fast or I'm too late
and his footfall fades as he moves on
to the elsewhere of lower Duke Street along the harbor.
It happened: what I woke and waited for,
just the two of us and the garbageman,
trundling past in his city-size compactor,
before the deer head off wherever they go.
I say he runs, but it should be "he ran";
he isn't here this year;
maybe he's running later now, or elsewhere.
The dew will stain my slippers
when I go out in a while to grab the *Morning Sun*
in its blue plastic sleeve
from under the peegee that was gored
by a buck in rut last fall.
And even later at the Clavinova
(you're not an early riser,
even if you're top-notch, Tityrus)
you'll noodle over that blessed Chopin étude
(at night your fingers on the keys
resound like raindrops through the wall),
arpeggios watering the border

as I weed and worry and waste the day.
The wisteria was unbelievable this spring,
lavender tresses like a psychedelic Rapunzel's,
intoxicating clumps of edible petals
falling everywhere, and the lobelia
in the bowl the nymphs raise over their heads
like caryatids in training
in the statue I set at the end of the arbors
was a blue-purple exclamatory smudge
till it got leggy and had to be replaced.
Now an ivy geranium's hot lashes,
thin-petalled, almost coral blooms,
cascade down to the ferns;
they look like pom-poms from the porch,
where I sit pretending to read but mainly looking,
    plotting what to change and how.
The bee balm and the ferns
have filled out under the buddleias,
the butterfly bushes,
which are taller than the statue now:—
so many species, all intent on attracting
the only insects that we truly love.
Charles has given us two kinds of toad lily
to plant among them (but they didn't make it,
somehow his transplants seldom take;
my fault, I'm sure). Meanwhile those inimical
wisteria shoots keep fingering among the ferns.
I cut them back, more brutal every year.
I want it where I want it, nowhere else.
But the indomitable old rootball
is here to teach us all there is to know
about keeping going.

Dave's boat with its toy American flag
waving in the face of all our mayhem
sits by the barn, still waiting to be launched
far too late this plaguey spring.
It's there half-hidden by the trash walnut
that just showed up behind the hedge
he planted to protect us
from the backyard mess next door.
Not all that long ago it was a sapling
I could have pulled up in the night,
no one the wiser.
I almost did, in fact, but chickened out;
now it's an intrusion to contend with,
eavesdropping over the hedge,
contributing its yellow tennis ball–size fruits
filled with date-brown paste,
another part of the scrawny picture.
Near it is the escape from the paulownia,
the Empress Tree behind the Painter's house.
When I knew even less than I do now,
I thought the enormous shield-shaped leaves
manspreading by a rotting fishing boat
were just some weed that they kept hacking back.
Then James, who is a veritable gardener,
set me straight. Dave persuaded them
to cart the boat away,
but now their handsome foursquare barn's
at risk of disassembling,
with no panes in some of the windows.
Last week I trimmed the bushes
on the side we see from the kitchen
so bridal wreath spills onto the driveway
for its own luxuriant brief life.

The barn is picturesque for now;
before long it could be in trouble.
Dave and I worry over it,
and the other boat on the front lawn
in its blue tarpaulin. If only they
would let him move it to behind the barn.
There have been times I've thought
of calling up the Painter
who lives across the street and saying,
"Let's go halvesies,"
let's buy the boat
and give it to some worthy cause
the way you can donate your car to cancer.
But it's an heirloom.
Last year there was a party in the yard:
the whole family, several generations,
tore the tattered caul off the old boat
and soaped and rinsed it down. We thought:
They're selling it! But no.
The blue tarp is a banner,
that got changed for a less obtrusive,
anodyne gray Mylar.
No, it's a pennant,
telling us we live where people work,
or used to, on the water (not our neighbors, though).
Secretly, I like it.

AND THE SWAN IS GONE
from her nest on the bank
which her swain kept
so faithfully and tenderly

we don't know
how many of their cygnets made it
but like enough we'll see them later
out in the bay

and last week's hairless
bunny babies vacuum-packed
under the dead narcissus leaves
that the ground pulsed with
in the bed below the windows
are gone too
out in the clover somewhere
doing their thing

hard-ass spring's
inalterably
scheduled arrivals
beach plum last week
now exhausting
pungent wild roses
endless seduction
come-on beauty
all its *seme*
heedlessly
spento assieme.

Do you think the Burtons understand
(of course they do, unconsciously)
I have designs on the back lawn
where they store their lobster pots
for my *hortus conclusus*, the secret garden
I'm planning for you

behind a hedge of alternating
rose of Sharon, pink, then white
with raspberry swirl ice cream centers—
and Diana, with the purest, biggest,
whitest blooms of all, like the one that lines
the drive that's half the way down Village Lane.
Or the hornbeam hedge
that Juan installed
in Denise's garden, shades of Granada,
stark sentinels in the heart of town;
or else more privet, with its sticky flowers
that smell semeny in late June.
You'll amble down the brick walk in your flip-flops
on one of those occasions
when you venture outdoors, Tityrus,
under the wisteria, with maidenhair
ferns on the left and lavender (Provence)
and *Lamiastrum* on the right,
then under the small arbor
with its own complement of ferns and irises
(the old German brown ones Jared gave me
came in beautifully this spring,
after two years' acclimatizing,
though the ferns can crowd them out).
You'll turn left at the buddleia
huddled around the statue,
open the imaginary gate,
and come into the world I've made for you.

Remember the hidden close in Little Compton,
behind the sea fields where you were eaten alive
by lobster mosquitoes?
Inside those nondescript brick walls
we happened on a miniature oasis

out of the Arabian Nights,
a tranquil pool bordered by lilies and dahlias
(Why do the English say *daylia?* So annoying.
Dahl *was* Swedish, after all, not "Dale"),
protected from the unrelenting Atlantic ocean wind
that stunts the trees there.
(The planes and maples on Middle Road out here
have been hacked so the electric wires
can run right through them.)
It wasn't the flowers in that little bower
that made it magic;
they were everyday, if truth be told.
It was their hiddenness,
the serendipitous surprise of their just being there,
that made that garden unforgettable,
a little pleasure dome we happened on
and hanker after, even now.
My hidden garden will be something else:
a porch, a dressing room, an outdoor shower
(like F and M's on Shelter Island),
a grill for all the meals you'll cook *al fresco*,
a screen porch where you can be safe
from your tormentors. And in the corners,
late-flowering crape myrtles,
my favorite trees,
shades of the South here at their northern bourn
(they don't grow across the Sound;
Skip always claimed that Oyster Ponds
was Southern at heart)—and broad borders
east and west, graystone pool and statuary
(ancient, mossy), maybe vegetables
(no need for fences here);
or, better yet, fruit trees
in flawless grass: simplicity.

I have no sense of how to make my Eden;
it's overstuffed with far too much already.
I can only learn by trial and error,
which is how I do everything.
"Knit one, purl two," my grandmother used to say—
feeling my way as Vita did along
the "long Grave path you planned
as not your life you planned."
Think of all the plants I squander
every summer, so spendthriftily.
Where are the foamflowers of yesteryear?
Where's the soapwort that Charles gifted us
more than once? They're ghosting us;
will they emerge to mock us when we're history?
But how else could I do it?
I'm no learned horticulturist
whiling away the nonexistent
snowdrift evenings (though I do recall them),
nodding over catalogues and whiskey
by the fire, growing annuals from seed
like Charles or Jamaica,
fussing over their cold frames.
Why do our morning glories
always fail? Why am I so bad at clematis?
I'm just another summer amateur,
ripe for the condescension of the buxom
Helen Hokinson ladies or their daughters,
or gracile men dueling Latin nomenclatures,
doling out a few safe specimens
but not their darkest secrets.
Mac sent me *Salvia guaranitica*
from Virginia last spring
as if it were *sui generis*, a rarity.
But I have good old normal

black-and-blue and purple salvia.
What makes *guaranitica* so special?
Does it winter over? Come on, Mac,
I thought you were a pro.
(This year's yellow-orange crocosmia
are another story,
though they don't show so well in the far bed.)

Vita was the greatest pro of all.
Vita Sackville-West
of Sissinghurst White Garden fame,
Virginia Woolf's great passion,
model for Orlando,
whose poems *The Land* and *The Garden*,
unread today, define a certain
elegiac English land-love,
prophetic of our overheating world:
"Heavy July. Too rampant and too lush;
High summer, dull, fulfilled, and satiate,
Nothing to fear, and little to await.
The very birds are hush . . .
And those aggressive indestructible
Bores, the herbaceous plants, that gladly take
Whatever's given and make no demand
Beyond the careless favour of a stake;
Humble appeal, not arrogant command,
Like some tough spinster, doughty, duteous,
All virtue and no charm. . . .
Moderate beauty, yet insidious.
England, as douce as any woman's muff.
Where is the violence, the shrilly-voiced
Cicada of the arid plain?" (Not here,

but everywhere else, it seems, this year.)
Follow "as with steps obedient and slow
Homeward I turn, and to the tool-shed go . . ."
and laying down the law: hear, hear:
"Gardens should be romantic, but severe."
She was the Virgil of a world
about to evanesce, a Rilke of regret
(whom Auden called
"the Santa Claus of loneliness").
It was like Forster's greenwoods
—or gone already, as this one will be.
(Her grandson said the gardeners
had to reset everything she planted.
She sounds like me; was Vita a black thumb?)
This will all be gone, if not in my own time,
in yours, or in another hundred years.
But don't say that it won't be mourned;
don't say these views of tree and leaf
and lawn and road and field won't live
incised on someone's retina.
Aren't they afterimages themselves
of something more idyllic, simpler, greener,
that imaginary bower of perfect peace,
the first garden, the Horatian *rus*?
We could do far worse than to heed Vita.

The greatest gardeners in these parts,
as almost everywhere, have left no trace
(that's the way, stealth necromancy,
gelatin clouds that float above the shore
before they dissipate, or almost do).
Dwight Ripley and Rupert Barneby,

eccentrics made immortal
in Doug Crase's captivating *Both*,
fell in love at Harrow in the twenties.
After adventures and vicissitudes
(Beverly Hills, Wappingers Falls)
they washed up in a handsome foursquare
Greek Revival mansion on the Sound
a few miles down the road in Greenways,
thanks to their East Madgwick friend,
the abstract painter Theodoros Stamos,
best known now for having cheated
his friend Mark Rothko's children
out of part of their inheritance.
You can just see Stirling House today,
named for a local rill, I think,
overgrown, forlorn in spider-scrub
along the Middle Road.
Rupert and Dwight were misfits, loners,
like so many plantsmen. Dwight,
the scion of a railroad fortune,
was handsome, insolent, alluring, fey.
Peggy Guggenheim was a one-time lover,
and, more often, the buff taxi driver.
Early on he bankrolled
penniless Hungarian Tibor de Nagy's
gallery, that congeries of oddballs
no one else would show that morphed
into the later New York School
and helped to forge our city's sweetest style.
Dwight made eerie, lunar colored
pencil drawings of the xerophytes that he and Rupert
stalked in the Sonoran Desert,
naming species for themselves and their friends—
Lesquerella barnebyi, Gilia ripleyi, etc.,

English Rupert was the scientist,
"the most accomplished legume taxonomist
since Bentham," Doug asserts
authoritatively, and who can argue?
Disinherited when he fell for Dwight,
Rupert followed him to Moloch, and the rest is history,
and of great consequence for botany.
He grew old in a grace-and-favor flat
at the New York Botanical Garden,
where he'd catalogued species
for thirty years (word has it he was into leather, too,
though Doug doesn't venture there, alas).
Nothing survives of the rock garden
built from concrete blocks behind the house,
which Linc Foster called "a modern Alhambra."
Rupert described it as "a defence against
the almost Australian pullulation
of coneys and . . . the cruel northwesterlies
which sweep down from Poluninland"
—a hat-tip, presumably, to a frostbitten
Arctic colleague. Yes, it can be bleak
in Oyster Ponds in winter,
although the iceboat racing on Hallock's Bay,
back when there was ice, was really cheery,
with bonfires, flasks, and blankets,
the kids on skis barely holding on
to the speeding sterns that whipped across
the rough gray wavy surface.
But then a two-ton rock crushed Rupert's drawing hand.
Then Dwight died of cirrhosis
in Greenways Hospital in '73.
There was no one to hand on their obsessions to,
the way that Vita and Frank Cabot could,
or Iris Origo's daughters at La Foce.

Recently, a trunkful of Dwight's drawings
showed up in the house next door
and was exhibited in Greenways—
to small notice, I'm afraid.
Now another trove of madcap fantasies,
birdcages, travel posters, flowers,
has been found in a locked room.
It seems a local fisherman
who shared the house with Dwight and Rupert
when they moved on moved in
with their neighbor
and dragged Dwight's trunks along.
But gardens, unlike drawings,
go with their makers to the other place.
Nothing hovers; names perhaps at most.
Vita's tourist-trap White Garden is a simulacrum.
We crane our necks, inveigling a past,
a lusciousness, a cloying charm.
Richard and I went down once to Great Dixter
in search of . . . what?—
a soupçon, a snapshot's-worth, I guess,
of the late genial Christopher Lloyd's
gift for making scenes with leaves and blossoms.
And what we saw impressed us mightily,
May's profusion, row on row on row.
But was it Christopher's handiwork we saw—
or brooding Thor's, his manager and heir,
whose smoldering looks
the garden queens lapped up?

WE WATCHED THE VETCH AND MILKWEED
come alive in the meadow
what felt like overnight

and now the redwing blackbirds'
breastplates are being overmatched
by the ditch lilies
in the honeysuckle sweetness
of Narrow River Road
(though nothing
like the privet
when it gets to flowering)

the arbor
and the vineyard
the begonias that the deer don't eat (so far)

the lame rabbit
and the little plot
under the kitchen window—

Tudo, don't be vexed, don't kvetch
that this will all be underwater
fifty years from now.
The fact what seems eternal's
not eternal makes it
all the more lovely.

This afternoon a row of low clouds hangs
over Connecticut:
heavy there, but there is brightness here.
You point out blotchy rainstorms
on the far shore like a Nolde—
are they coming our way?
Dave and I have been wondering
what might happen if the vineyard vanished.
Would it be plowed under, turned into a lawn,

or, worse, a house lot (is it big enough)?
It's for ever in our eyes,
but Dave grew up two doors away;
he was here when Dr. No
conceived it thirty years ago or more.
To him it's new.
The primal-seeming gnarly Oyster Ponds
woods that scramble over what were fields
is nature saying, *Hold on a minute;
you won't recognize the place.*
We've seen the God shots
when the peninsula was only farms,
thirty-three of them from shore to shore,
and, Louisa says, "You couldn't give them away."
Freddie and Sylvia, when they bought their house,
could glimpse the back bay winking from their yard.
The Sculptor and his wife, who live on Green Street,
took down a perfectly serviceable
shingle house behind them
and another one across the street,
to encourage the illusion they're protected
from encroachment by the likes of us.
We're the beneficiaries
of their rage for things
to be what they weren't.
I want to go back, too,
to the pristine world I never knew—
vicious winters, moaning wind
in virgin forests, wolves, bears,
tires with snow chains, dayslong blizzards—
where we all came from
before air-conditioning and brush fires
and instant messaging spoiled everything.
The Sculptor lives—or lived—here now;

the time of artists
camping in the wilderness is done for.
Now there's just this semi-suburb
they're trying to reel back into countryside.
Don't they know that it will all revert
eventually, like the Chernobyl forests
those huge herds stream through silently?
Walt and Sandy, when they built
their jewel box above the marsh,
went to enormous trouble to root out
invasives so that their wild-seeming place
would be wild with native species only
—except for the endemic Russian olives,
neither Russian nor olive,
though they have the silver underleaves
we love in oleaster, silverberry,
artemisia, helichrysum (licorice plant
to you and me; Jane says it's excellent
for filling in when you need to fill in);
and that metallic shimmer in the garden,
dusty miller, which has been known
to winter over in the peony bed,
is daylit moonlight. They can see
Montauk from upstairs, where Winslow Homer's
sharp New England uncle
got rich stealing land from the Montauketts
and building summer cottages with Stanford White.

The view from the Architect's roof deck up the road
is even more spectacular;
Montauk is much farther to the left
of Gardiner's Island than you might imagine:
windblown water fields and islands,
gentle distances, Block Island

hovering unseen to the east.
Our Covid voyage there (it took two ferry rides
via New London) was Homeric:
glittering, churning Buzzards Bay,
mythic Ithaka rising out of the fog—
though it, too, is more suburban now,
with wind turbines off the lighthouse,
and the black and blue regatta in the Ponds
was an outrage. We biked the whole perimeter,
which you thought was a little much
(if only I could do it now).
Still, it's my notion of an island.
But when you take the causeway to the State Beach
with Gardiner's Bay on your left
and Hallock's Bay on your right,
the ridged blue water in its sleeve of green,
the irrigators rolled across the fields beyond,
the water trucks
scattering feeble rainbows at the crops
(can this really be efficient?)
this might be heaven,
except the greenheads take a piece of your leg
when you stop to adjust your shorts.
Who's across the water in Green River
where the Pollocks and de Koonings were
and Frank is buried? Who haunts Louse Point?
(We made a pilgrimage
to the Springs cemetery last year
and came upon a fox and a lone doe
among the pines and lichened graves
and a Coke bottle
on Frank's simple, perfect stone.)
When I was younger I would have biked here
every day the way Suzanne does, to keep honest,

but I can still (just) manage the twelve miles,
even if I'm knackered afterwards
and my bum knee complains.
I ride the Middle Road past the Sculptor's fields,
and the reed forest on the Loring farm
beyond Narrow River is a savanna.
No mangroves here, no manatees,
but something lurks here, too;
is it an ocelot,
feral and hieratic
out of Rousseau? Not just the constant
pairs of swans and geese
that ply the river's dirty finger
too near the goat farm's putrid effluent
and the cornfield where we saw the fox
devouring something and gamboling off,
his tail a flaming prick saluting the sun.
Something more mysterious
howls silently at night,
moaning beneath the breeze—
is it a cousin of the skunk, the vole
that stole the peaches I left out on the lawn chair?
Or those diamond eyes that fix on me
when I take out the garbage?

THE ROSE
is close:
for renovation
or recuperation
or else it simply needs
a brief vacation
from all that we expect of it:

to be ever-dewy
ever-budding
open to disclose
the secret
of its luscious
velvet heart
so pure
we just might
have to take a bite

being so
accommodating
has to be
exasperating
when all it really
wants to do
perhaps
is furl up
curl up
for some beauty
sleep

who knows?
whatever gives
for now
the rose
is close

You can't buy faded rugs like these.
They need to be aged by feet and sun and house dust
and humidity, and who has time for that?
(I guess I do. Who but you has the years
that it will take this tree to rise and fill out?)

"Plant your trees now," Alton used to say,
but the ones I planted
put roots down elsewhere.
And Alton took a powder long ago.
To get something this experienced,
this trod-upon and faded, like my faded beauty,
you have to put in decades. Think about it,
you who are fresh as a daisy.
Examining my face—was it Cocteau
who said that mirrors are the doors of death?—
I find it's not *all* bad, so far, except the wrinkles,
and how one side droops a little.
A tan can help conceal the ravages,
if it doesn't underline them;
and my Covid beard, the first beard of my life,
made me look more mischievous
(some say *mischievious*;
some say *folage*, even worse;
some say *restauranteur; for Jane and I*)
till it made me older.
But avert your eyes from the dad bod;
there's no way to hide a life of indulgence,
the evening pink drinks that we love;
no number of the sit-ups I don't do
will undo the wreckage.
I take it as it comes (as if I had a choice),
"I laugh when I can and weep when I must,"
says Juan, my most Horatian philosopher.
There are days I feel like Crusoe
camped out with Friday on our quasi island.
Friday in the kitchen on a call
with three o'clock coffee,
or noodling that Schumann *fantaisie* at the Clavinova,
trying to get up to Pollini speed.

Well, we all have immoderate ambitions.
The secret seems to lie in repetition,
letting the hands absorb their moves
and etch their neural trenches.
That's how you get to Carnegie Hall.
(Friday, when will we be there again,
rapt and wrapped in cream and gold and plush?
—In fact we made it, just the other day,
and it was otherworldly, majestic as always.—
Majesty survives, but where you find it.
You have to seek it out, it doesn't
grab you by the beard the way it used to.)
But beauty does, and without explanation,
a primary phenomenon, says Goethe.

I'm putting my queer shoulder to the wheel
here in fish-shaped Paumanok,
hanging on for dear life before climate collapse.
Who remembers the fire that ran,
impetuous in the world's veins?
(Today it's out the window, with no warning.)
But that was then, when I was green
(I was young like you, but so much greener;
you were always older, always knew).
The world was so confusing: rage and turmoil,
as it had to be. The world was cruel.
We let our hair grow long and hated war,
especially if it meant we'd have to fight.
We looked out for Number One,
and see what happened: see what's happening.
(Darryl says the young are angry
because they know that we had fun.)
We're leaving lots of empties in the rental.

MY CONSCIENCE IS CLEAR

I look in the mirror and stare at the years
peering back out of a wrinkling face.
I stare at the screen as the crisp words appear
that used to spurt from a passionate pen.
I even look down at my waist when I dare.

Where did it go to, I mutter in wonder,
when did the guilt and the anguish and fear
take a run for the door and abandon me here?
How did I end up so old and so free?
I don't remember the first thing about them.
That's what I mean when I say that my conscience is clear.

Pretend peace: birdsong and the once-blue boat
(dull now in its inert aluminum shroud)
across the driveway. I used to hack the weeds back
under the neighbors' spindly yew
while their tenant was at work.
What was I avoiding, doing that?
There's always something to shy away from,
to not own up to, to not look at,
like the new house in the tree farm
or that gash in the woods on Middle Road
that soon will be a building site.
And the huge boulders on the lawn
on Deeter's Road that were bulldozed out of the ground
and left there to show us
what ground it is we walk on, what the glacier
raked out of the Sound and left us with.

A better morning comes to pass,
sunlight buttered on the grass.
No one ever treated us so gently
as these green-going-to-yellow hands
fanned out where we walk.
If I look out this window from this height
the vineyard's like a flag by Johns
fluttering its long yellow-green stripes,
dark crevices between the sunstruck ones.
Someone's jogging on their morning run,
the deer were prancing on the lawn last night,
the way they almost never do.
The buddleias' batons above the privet
consort with the rose of Sharon's violet blooms,
not my favorite color but I'll take it
because what else is there to do?
No magenta-centered panna cotta blossoms
crowning, then falling every day
onto the lawn and into the new bed
the way the wisteria's wispy intermittent
second swags poke out of the arbor,
sad excuse for a poet's fillet.
The vineyard leaves reach up like dancing hands
while the grapes hang down;
the guys will come and raise the nets
near the end of the season,
to save the ripe fruit from the birds,
a curtain falling in the *entr'acte*
(except they're cranked up from below
so their gathered bulk won't shade the vines).
I want color—hot late-summer reds and oranges
and whites and yellows,
a second front to stave off what's ahead,
which is why I planted the border

along the back hedge,
getting semi-serious, semi-greedy,
though I'm daunted
by the responsibility,
the time and attention, the tsuris,
the certain rout.
The seasons are cruel, yes,
and the deer are remorseless.
Let's try Milorganite; let's see
if it stops them (it does, for a night).
Jane advises I get Deer Defeat.
I do. I'm just another duffer
nattering on about humiliation:
you should have been here yesterday, last week.
As Skip said, quoting Henry Mitchell,
"A gardener's life is full of woe."

It's no secret everything we had
is slipping away—last night, this morning,
before you noticed, because you noticed.
I go out and survey what got eaten,
what needs pruning, not to mention
everything that's on my conscience:
those I didn't love or loved in error;
those I hurt, the endless gyre.
All those years barking up Andy's tree,
those eyes-averted blandishments,
his cool half love. What did he want?
We love the things we love for what they *were*,
Adam, and for who we were as well.
And now Saskia is gone.
And Page. And Jon, and Robbie now. And Star. And Jim:

BOOKWORMS

James Atlas (1949-2019)

It wasn't just the wide brown hazy view
of Castel Sant'Angelo in its Eastlake frame
and the stuffed peahen
you were humping across the Yard;
it was the raincoat and galoshes, too,
and your air of pulling a heist off,
intelligence poised like a harpoon.
But everything was sepia then
that wasn't Technicolor.
You, ringleader of the Bookworms,
gunning for the geezers in their fifties
who couldn't keep a fire alive,
but their suns enflamed the horizon.

Boar's Hill, our sonnet contests, Blueberry Hill,
Dwight's dacha with his pinup undie ads,
wives in the pool, wives in the mirror, kids—
we dove into the molehill, chasing our tails,
bowling for a strike
that might lift us into word heaven.
Your books were out-and-out nostalgia
for the old culture wars—the life-or-death ones.
No one clocked the dads the way you did,
irksome white guys nursing their resentments
like tumblers of Dewar's.

I don't know what happened to the peahen
but the castle still hangs in your dining room
where I've wolfed down a lifetime
of game birds in sepia sauce,
scanning the battlements of Eighty-First Street.

Your shelves are crammed with books, no room for others.
Who thrills to the old outrage,
who covets the brown furniture we lived by?
Where is word heaven, Jim?

Then there are the ways that Wendy feels,
about what I did, and didn't do,
our life I overturned, the love I left,
the cold, hard fact of it, the rock in the road.
There are things I tell to no one.
JL's poem where he writes,
"I was cruel" is his great moment.
"I was cruel": eyeball that for a lifetime.
My precious daughters needed to endure
my years of errancy:
the black hole of Brian, the detour with Bob
(not to mention Juan, and Neil, and Icarus).
They both said very little,
but their silence spoke volumes.
And soon the newest generation
will have ideas of their own.
Everyone's entitled to their feelings.
Lots of nights
I lie awake and catalogue my failures.

Joel, pull down thy vanity.
Or else, keep calm and carry on.
Never complain, like the Queen
with her marmalade sandwich and knife of an accent.
People are cruel to those who are unlike them,
scanning eyes they're anxious to be seen by,
shunning others, when it's them they need to love.

What I hope for, now that it's too late,
is absolution for my unforced errors
(Sheena says, Good luck with that).
Yet here you are, unblemished Tityrus.
Everybody understands
who the grown-up in this house is.
You came along at last when I knew what I was doing,
more or less. And here you are,
watering the border from the Clavinova,
giving me the life I don't deserve.

Guess what! I can open the front door.
Every now and then the thin key catches,
and air and light invade the hall.
We're in *and* out, the way I like it best,
new breezes visiting the rooms,
waving in health and vigor and refreshment.
I love to sleep with open doors,
my idea of glamping: nothing but a screen
between us and the night. Who's out there?
Who purloined my peaches?
And our sister deer, masticating placidly.
And God knows what else: night runners, avid eyes.
There's just too much to do—
take the bike ride, pick up the picture,
get the salmon. I think I'll go to Braun's.
Ann says they're better for fish from away,
while Charlie's better for the local catch.
(There were no bay scallops anywhere last year;
the water was too warm.)
I like a quarter of a watermelon, not a whole one;
otherwise, it rots in the refrigerator.

I'll get one when I go to Trimble's,
and Wickham's for peaches (and perhaps a donut hole)
and miss the crowds. We are the crowd,
the incomers.
We plopped ourselves down here
seven years ago (no, nine now, ten, eleven, twelve),
and put down our shallow roots,
crooked or straight. How do you establish roots?
People with veritable roots don't move.
A cat can look at a king because the king
is a cat with jewels and a pedigree.
But roots are constricting. We aren't horses.
Being Angus Duke who lives on Duke Street
isn't all that easy, maybe.
Maybe Angus, too, feels fraudulent,
not being the first Angus, the *real* Angus,
living off another's reputation
(or maybe he's just fine with it).
You can hear the reverent undertones
in Mona's voice when she allows
that she swims on the Sampsons' beach.
Some infrared mutation
changes us, we tell ourselves.
And if you don't have roots,
if you're a tumbleweed? It could be a blessing,
no ties you'd just as soon not have,
nothing to come to terms with,
to discard or make amends for
yet feel the lack of.
Rich people should be ashamed (as I'm ashamed
of my pretend peace, my happiness).

But all this will be underwater soon,
as, Tityrus, you love reminding me.

Will the causeway wash away
and Oyster Ponds become a real island?
I love the integrity of islands,
their self-sufficient little worlds
excise the unnecessary:
one grocery store with flaccid vegetables,
one depot where the newspaper shows up
two days late and if you're lucky you can scrounge
a can of tomatoes.
Couldn't we be happy there, worrying about nothing
but how to forage, which is what we do here?
Will it be Smithfield IGA or Greenways,
Fairview in a pinch (despite their politics),
Loring's or Sim's,
who sell (or used to) only what they grow.
I don't have the heart for CC's,
where every lettuce leaf is curated,
or Hands Down with its $70 chickens,
though Tina swears by them.
You have to draw the line somewhere;
I don't buy my groceries at Costco,
though Charles and the girls do
(maybe we should, too).
I do prize the Old Field reserve Chardonnay,
as unguent almost as a Californian—
sunlight buttered on the grass—
though their vines can't be very ancient
since it was only fifty years ago
that the Young Man of the Mountain and his bride,
with foolhardiness and grit,
set out to give this place new roots,
and made a world.

SUMMER AFTERNOON

the marsh grass bends
a little with the trees
which have started drying out
whatever you say
now that the Virginia creeper
is finally definitively red

and the field of Queen Anne's
lace you loved
has been plowed under
and Hallock's Bay is cooler
since the rainstorm flooded the marsh
and the night is fine for sleeping
after all the humidity

it's been a perfect summer
with sun and water
and breath and quiet
and grapes beginning to darken on the arbor
and early leaves
that soon enough will be filtering
into the most beautiful words in the language
whatever you say

Freddie has published several books
about the early days of Oyster Ponds.
In one we see Jane Hubbard, thrilled
to finally get to travel to Southampton.
Earlier she'd missed the boat to Jamesport
twenty miles up island,
but went there with her husband later on.

How desperate these East End women were
for a taste of Riverhead sophistication,
or New London or Fall River even,
where the steamers went
so you could catch the train to Boston.
The old road from Huntington to Montauk
you sometimes see in Whitman exhibitions
was telegraph poles and saw grass
to the bleak horizon.
Today it's hours on the LIE
through Levittowns that once were farms
and the Sound was knee-deep in oysters,
heaps in the city shellfish emporia
(even then New Yorkers lived in restaurants).
Now people come out here from Huntington
and Farmingdale
and hang hoops above their asphalt driveways.
The new lanes off Middle Road
wind through fields to new suburbias
littering the shore.
Thank God we can avert our eyes—
what are eyes for but not to see?
But let's pause in praise
of the fierce brigade of lesbians
who used to guard the gates of Oyster Ponds,
the legendary Anne MacKay
with her pushpin map of local Sapphists
and all the other heroines
who fought the philistine developers
and kept the place an afterimage of itself,
a bower, an Eden, a safe place in plain sight
where they and we are free to be.
We used to see them sunning by the rocks
at Deeter's Cove late afternoons,

the way their progeny still do,
the Amazon emeritae retailing lore about
their Greatest Generation:
"Natalie went out to California
when she took the job at USC."
"No, when she and Emily split up"—
layers of underpainting, codes of feeling.
And their confreres the blue blazer set,
Stewart Johnson, publicist and curator,
who bought a fine old house in Greenways
and had it hauled on rollers up Cave Hill
to the longest view in Oyster Ponds.
Modestly courageous lives and loves:
who will write these unrecorded histories?

I've hung my garden tools on the wall under
    the arbor,
my trophies, my insignia of life and time.
Luckily, Dave approves and takes
a snapshot for his friends.
The grapevines climb so high this time of year
that I can barely even see Suzanne's.
Their tops are gold flames in the sun,
pennants in the gale before the storm,
deep green below. The guys arrive to spray
in their hazmat suits,
as if it were dangerous work;
it may well be, what with the bees
and the lethal stuff they use
to keep the weeds down
the way we used to do in Norfolk,
shamefully.

I watched the deer along the tree farm fence
tonight, I see them loping in the mystic dawn.
Later little planes and helicopters
hover like a Šašek illustration.
I have dawdled luxuriated reveled
in these happiness pounds
and too much is enough, as my mother used to say.
Where did she get her truculent
self-denying mild transgressive wit
that strikes me as so precious now?
Her Chicago feet, she used to call them,
since they were big and flat, I guess
(or were they?).
Was it her Depression child's unease,
her sense of never fully having her balance,
of being the unvalued older sister?
Did she inter her disappointment
under my grandmother's smothering cheer?
Only occasionally did it sound in the driveway
bright and brittle as a xylophone.
Where had my all-accepting mother gone?
Who else heard the hardness, the despair
that echoed then?
Why did she call my sister Arabella?
Why did I preserve these things
stored up and pondered in my heart till now?
What else got swept up from the cutting room floor?
My Christ's College prize book Milton
is more than fifty years old now,
a generation younger than her double
Keats and Shelley and John Masefield,
even more unread today than Vita.
He was Poet Laureate; Bellow won the Nobel Prize.
Who reads them now?

Her course books in their two-tone Thirties jackets,
"Cazenove Hall" scrawled inside in pencil,
are nearly a hundred. Old tomes, old alchemies
to crack the backs of with forced fingers rude.
Don't you love the must of summer volumes?
I adore old books, not rare ones.
Saskia gave me a foxed Oxford Herbert
from the war years—God knows where she found it—
that is a deeply prized possession.
I have a first-edition Leopardi, also,
"shared" with an Italian friend,
that sits like Vesuvius smoking on my shelf,
its leathery paper stained with insect tracks.
Who could read it?
It's not for the mortal likes of us.

JL made a joke of the old story
about how he aspired to be a poet
but selfish Ezra cut him to the quick,
enjoining him to be his publisher instead,
which he did, heroically.
Yet in his later years he found a way back
to his first love and the work just flowed,
in hemistichs and other arcane forms
lifted from Adelaide Crapsey and like sources.
His poems have a foursquare honesty;
like Pound's they derive from their classic masters.
JL was chuffed at being called
"il Catullo americano"
in an Italian review. His view of love
was chivalrous and formulaic,
charmed, relaxed, lubricious
in an old-style, gentlemanly way.
It was like his crew cut and knit ties,

emblems of a gone patrician ease.
They took their Latin and their Greek for granted
and were in love with the idea
of love and loving, always being in love.

We need rain. I water for literal hours,
hauling the sprinkler back and forth
yet things still poop out by midafternoon.
New plants fold like fans till they take root,
or don't. When I was stuck in town
I used to get the twins to water for me
and Troy would text, "It took us forty-five minutes!"
meaning they needed a raise.
Then they started helping Dave
on his boat; no more watering.
I went at the old apple tree the other morning
with my rusty handsaw before it started drizzling
and kept at it. There was a lot of deadwood
lower down, only a few apples came in up high.
But the black locusts at the back of the yard
are high and proud, with shapely complementary crowns.
They're said to be invasives, but I cherish them
for how they shelter and place us,
though now the left one's lost its top,
the way the arborvitae did in yet another storm,
so they're a little less than perfect now,
a little less a pair.

And what happened to the cimicifuga?
(Jenny wisely calls it cohosh,
so much less intimidating.)
I planted it with thalictrum, meadow rue,

the way Jim Heber used to do in Sharon,
enlaced old married couple
to be spied on from the kitchen window,
chatting across the air.
The meadow rue with lacy pink florets
is thriving still, but the snakeroot vanished.
Actaea, the plantsmen call it.
This year I see the deer have nipped its blooms.
I need to bring it back; these plants
deserve each other.
Cultivate your garden,
Tityrus tells me when I moan about the world,
watching the daily cataclysms on TV,
tsunamis, famine, murders, rapine,
statues pulled down, people disappeared,
families dissected, freedoms vaporized.
Was every time as terrible as this,
but people didn't know it?
We see the mayhem nonstop on our feed,
like milch cows, hitched to our pails.
But what is there to do
but lament, decry, resist, protest?
And hope somehow to be forgiven
for everything we haven't done
(and, maybe more, for what we have),
while we fret in our caves?
When do the accounts get reconciled?
"Keep out of the sun," a wise man said,
"but don't blame the sun."

I keep thinking I see something
in the corner of my eye.
Was it a bird that flitted past,

or did something dive into the bushes?
Was there a death that we don't know about:
that catbird lying at the foot of one of the lilacs
with a reddish brown dash under his tail feathers,
as if he hadn't wiped?
And there's turkey poop on the terrace this morning.
You keep saying, "There's a bunny," but I miss him.
You said you saw a mouse among the peonies
but I think it might have been a vole.
They've infested Oyster Ponds, I hear;
Tina's lawn was ruined. I always miss your bunny,
though they're so many,
cavorting on the lawn at dusk,
flirting, murdering the phlox,
and the new Joe Pye Weed stalks.
They're living in the privet hedge this year.
They used to nest, and maybe they still do,
under the Clavinova window; I'd find hanks of fur
when I cleaned out the bed in spring.
I love to see the garden through the windows,
spying on the border from behind,
illicit luscious backstage butt
in the shaving mirror. The bathroom window's
where we have our best view of the vineyard,
or one of them. Al'an did a sketch of it
we hung above the toilet,
fluid, fleeting, blotchy, out of focus
(not his memory, but maybe ours).
No, I think I half saw something else.
A shadow moved from right to left,
an intimation, half-imagined.
What have I missed? Is it you I've missed,
or one of the others?

Shadows in the late-day kitchen
where all I hear are birdcalls
and a couple with their dog out in the street.

I'M STARTING TO FEEL KINDER
toward my old poems,
more forgiving of
their quiverings and sap,
their anxious ironies.
The poor things were so desperate
to be presentable
in bow tie and bluchers,
serving up their truths with oven gloves
while the river ran on.
They kept it up
and took it on the chin,
revolutionary-conventional,
dutiful, and dull.

But they sat at the window
Saturday mornings watching
who it was who came to see
the bearded guy across the street
and wondering.

The pivoine plate,
peony etched blue on simple biscuit
that I got for you on Etsy,
was advertised as flat, but is
just the slightest bit concave, of course,

so your cake sags a little in the middle
like the gorgeous one you made
for our summer lunch under the arbor.
Jim and Stevie and the rest of Rancho Obsesso
trundled down from the Hill
(they can see both Sound *and* Bay,
the ultimate cachet in Oyster Ponds),
for a sunstruck Renoir afternoon.
But you're not baking up a storm today;
you're at work in the city,
leaving me here in our love nest
(it's our love nest, even when I'm here alone).
On my ride tonight the mist was clearing,
the atmosphere still heavy. It was cool:
I couldn't choose
whether to turn back at the end of Narrow River,
retrace my route and see the water
from the other way as we usually do
—a wholly different ride, as Karen writes—
(they call it a river
but it's just a finger of the estuary);
or should I go ahead
and take the Middle Road to Village Lane,
our Guermantes Way, past the embattled
Epaminondas farm
(he wanted to raise a barn and have events;
there were objections; now it's up for sale),
past the Cave Hill Road
and the farm where they sell logs, $5.00 per pile
("pairpilay," we always tell each other),
the tree farm and the berry man
(who's usually been closed since Covid;
I'm afraid he may be gone), then Jones Road
and the Edward Hopper service station,

where Bill, the uncrowned mayor of Oyster Ponds
—his father played pro ball which makes him
a cherished town celebrity—
dispenses car talk, poetry, life lessons;
the inn (*Is it for sale?* no,
it was sold); the firehouse
(they have—or used to have—a pancake breakfast *and* a pig
roast); the school and tennis courts,
the Congregational Church that recently
marked three hundred fifty years of worship;
the huge stump at the head of Deeter's Road
you think they should take down (I don't);
and the obelisk where Village Lane begins,
incised with the names
of the illustrious dead who battled slavery;
then down past the Hysterical Society,
as my mother used to call it,
and the other war memorials:
Vietnam, Korea, World Wars One and Two,
sprinkled among the postcard-perfect houses,
past the little yacht club on the jetty,
to come around at last to Duke Street?
I took my chances, risked the ferry traffic
that slices through the village twice an hour
and will not slow (*Would I? Would you?*)
for an old duffer struggling across the road.
Today for once I missed it,
at six o'clock on a weekday August afternoon,
my summer aura full,
limb-loosened, sated,
I rolled home in tranquility, though not with you.

And the jellyfish are back in the Sound;
it's August and they reappear like clockwork.

For a few years we convinced ourselves
they'd moved on—which shows
just how short our bandwidth is.
Out in deep water, Dave reports,
the six-hundred-pound leatherback
turtles show up (from where?) to feast on them,
but not enough to make a difference.
I want to watch them
eat up those red-centered men-of-war
that terrorize us and are destined, some predict,
to own the posthistoric seas.
And the old blue hydrangea,
the one Lorraine sagely wouldn't let me replace,
has bloomed now after years of dormancy,
enormous blue Nantucket globes;
the deer must have missed its buds this year,
but not the oak leaf that I planted several years ago.
Maybe they nipped *it* in the bud instead,
or maybe it's just temperamental.
It's grown up to where the bridal wreath
used to hide the windows from the street,
and anyway their fig-like leaves
are as beautiful as any flower;
they'll cover any man's equipment.
Charles says it blooms on old wood
and someone must have pruned it
(I bet I know who: me).

I went outside just now
to try and see the biplane overhead,
or was it a copter castling on the leg
from East Hampton to Manhattan?
So much annoyance, so much class resentment,
and when I wake in the morning

to what I want to think is stillness,
whole undertones I sometimes wish I couldn't hear
(so take out your hearing aids!).
We're expecting thunderstorms today;
the air is watery, stirred up,
the birds are hiding. Something's up,
we're waiting for an end,
a few more weeks, a few more months,
a few hundred thousand more
invisibly revolving years.
I'm starting to imagine city life,
our comings and our goings, our routines,
our loves and habits;
where to hang Ying Li's hypnotic
Memory of Oyster Ponds,
so we can be here while we're there;
our city life, our city love,
and the myth of return.
The hazmat men are here today
to cut the grape leaves back
now that the sun is weaker.
I did the same thing yesterday,
thinning the leaves in the arbor so the peonies
can have more light before their own leaves shrivel
(but now they're getting eaten by the deer,
even though it's said they're poisonous)
and the hummingbird can find his feeder.
The apices of the vines
aren't as pointed or as yellow
as the day before yesterday.
The grapes are darkening, too,
their energy condensing down below.
Soon—aren't they late this year?—
the black nets will be raised

to keep away the ravening birds.
We're not here for harvest normally;
I always hoped for harvest
but something always harried us away;
besides I dread incipience, the shutting down,
the cooling, the decline
of the light I thrive on. (The dread begins
the morning of the solstice.)

Oh, he was always x and y,
and I was z and a,
and our tormented back-and-forth
continues to this day.

Or did. Or does for me. This gentle season,
moment of exhalation, summit over,
though we don't want to know it yet,
but the bowing crickets tell you
and the strafing Canada geese
and the Virginia creeper
which finally is definitively red,
etched onto the oak on Narrow River,
but you don't have to listen,
don't see it yet if you don't want to,
and who wants to? Next year's planting
goes on covertly, or ought to.
We know we have to coexist with them,
why can't they be reasonable?
There's plenty else to go for
besides the few things that I want to grow;
the mile-a-minute needs shutting down,
for instance; it's only been around since '89
but it's run wild like kudzu.
Can't they home in on that?

(I always thought that it was *hone*,
till someone set me straight.) Meanwhile,
I'm finally planting the new bed:
Joe Pye Weed, black-eyed Susan,
illegal loosestrife
lifted from a roadside in Connecticut,
goldenrod behind the tall late-summer daubs of orange,
my beloved Mexican sunflowers
(*Tithonia,* they call them),
and the grasses that the Architect
let me dig up from the fields around his house
that feel like Jamaica. Charles's ironweed
grows to eighteen feet,
but not here (like the foamflowers
that didn't come back
at the base of the statue,
or last year's pink monarda).
We have to hope for next year.
We have to widen the bed and find a way
to keep them out. (Did I mention, by the by,
that Mac's *Salvia*
is putting on a tremendous show—
delicate pale blue floret
racemes that rise and rise,
another gift that keeps on giving,
the only pure blue in the garden
above the Clavinova bed.
It makes the *Verbena bon* look almost vulgar.
Mac, I was wrong—another sin: forgive me.
It is a very precious thing indeed.)

INSTRUCTIONS TO MY EULOGIST

I'd like to be remembered
for my sensibility and sadness,
my uncharted depths, my self-effacing manners—
not my selfishness and impatience,
my gluttony and servile pride.
I'd like to be called out for my constancy
in spite of appearances,
for conquering some of my failings,
and be absolved of the rest.

Please mention the tough row that I had to hoe
and how uncomplainingly I bore my burdens.
Overlook my squirrelly neatness,
my snobbery and imperfect
personal hygiene.

Recollect the little things
like cleaning out the art cart,
not my hobbling obsessions,
though a wise friend said
they're right there on your face
for all to see.

Lastly I hope
you'll find it in your heart to say
he made his little corner
habitable for a while and then moved over
and made room for others.

The turkeys process like prelates
threshing, winnowing

shaven from unshaven, saved from unsaved.
This year three mothers and twelve chicks—
I've learned the toms have posses of their own—
lumber up onto the tree farm fence,
then lumber down and hustle over the road
to fan out agitated on the lawn.
The young'uns poke their necks out as they peck
the same way their mothers do.
Last year they amazed us,
squawking and flapping up onto a maple branch
at the sight of a deer.
But Beau's men lopped it off
when they trimmed up the arborvitaes;
where will they find their safety now?
Later I learn the family sleeps
in the big trees behind Sandro's,
wobbling down the runway of the lawn
and trundling up onto the roof,
then into the high branches,
where they immediately settle down.

These green going to yellow . . .
Marvin's ginkgoes,
spindly trees that are the last to turn
on our city block. Their leaves fall late,
pulled down by snow or a rainy tantrum.
The noble trees stand watch like guardsmen
in the cavern of the street. Out here, though,
they're free to find their natural shape.
Who gets to do that? Very, very few;
and what's my natural shape
these days, I need to ask,
surely not the bum knees and crabbed fingers
that I share with my mother and her mother.

I used to play with the veins of Muffie's hands
and the charms on her bracelet;
my mother, too, had painful, knobby fingers
and mine are crumbling now, I'm told,
which is why I take the hydroxychloroquine,
which meant I had a nonsymptomatic case
the first time, if I did.
Think of all the jars you have to open,
all the other favors that I have to ask you.
Luckily there are some things
that I can still do with a little help,
things that I can do for you—for now.

Remember the doe
with the broken right front leg
who lived behind the barn
and hobbled around stoically
our first few years?
Had she been hit by a car,
like Phoebe, the girls' Irish terrier,
who ran right at a wheel
and limped for all her days?
Noble Hildegarde is history now;
they say they live five years,
or six. But there are always more
to take their place, always more and more.
We counted fourteen fawns
on the pond road the other night.
And there are more of us to them, no doubt:
they stare back myopically,
affronted at us intruders.
Mornings, once I've raised the shades,

I watch the sun announce from the northeast;
then the mystery fades
and the place stops being Brigadoon,
the mist flees and the silence gets infused
with an undertone of traffic
heading for the ferry.
But on the bus from Cutchogue yesterday,
I was sitting two feet higher up than normal,
and saw how nature's still in charge here:
water's everywhere,
the fields and vineyards own the inland,
while we hug the corrupted shore.
Sometimes we like to drive down to New Suffolk
and see the way the water meets the land there,
gentler because it's deep inside the Bay.
Snowball viburnum, Wickham's peaches, Wickham's
cherry pie jam—but best of all
Oysterponds Farm golden raspberry jam,
so hard to get
(they didn't even make it this past year).

The season's slow parade. And then it's over.
Tom likes Monty Don and so do we.
Monty Don's *Verbena bon*
floats above the border,
and the Japanese anemone I meant
to place among them: pert, four-petaled,
gold-centered second-story blooms
(cousin to Mac's *Salvia!*)—
much prized, too, by the deer—
but I never quite succeed in getting them
to work together (this year they were swallowed up
by the gooseneck loosestrife. They are *gone*).
And one time we came back from the city

to find the top of the taller arborvitae
had broken off in a storm and crashed on the lawn.
Charles showed me where the trunk
had split and weakened as it grew.
Now it's maimed two-thirds of the way up.
Its history is this,
valiant, wounded relic, holding on.
(If you didn't know it, maybe you won't notice,
you won't hear me talking to myself,
fitting my little tiles, my tesserae.)

Fred fell down the stairs.
After a maybe marginally
more than normally bibulous evening
he got out of bed at four
and turned right instead of left
on his way to the bathroom.
We heard a thud and there he was
in the hall by our door.
Stupidly, we put him back to bed,
then thought better of it
and took him to the emergency room
at Greenways Hospital,
which seems to specialize in weekend woes:
fishhooks in fingers
("I want to die," a young boy moaned to no one);
and then there was your cut lip, Tityrus,
when you fell off your bike on Deeter's Road
and had to have seven stitches—
hence the beard I love.
That Saturday an old dame from the Landing,
concerned about her dinner for her guests,

called during her transfusion
to make sure her daughter drained the potatoes.
Fred was fine, miraculously,
just a bit sore for a day or two
or three. People do it all the time,
the Greenways nurse informed us
matter-of-factly. We were set to go
by 5:30 as the sun showed up
to oil the rain-streaked roads.
Tityrus cooked us breakfast
and we all went back to bed.
Then there was the time that Alan thought
he was having a heart attack at lunch under the arbor
and it was off to Greenways again!
He wasn't, thank God, but it's all
the same to them, God bless 'em,
all in a day's or a night's work.
But Fred hasn't spent the night again,
though we put a gate up at the top of the stairs
for him and Luka.
Freddie, come back and exorcize your demons!

THE BOYS OF JUNIOR HIGH

What I loved about you, Randy Gallo,
beyond your sweetness and intelligence,
was how your basket canted
to fill the curve of your jeans.
Of course you were a shortstop:
pure all-American unself-consciousness.

And rail-thin, sunny, gentle Donnie Costa
lived in a mythic cabin in a bog.
I loved your cool dark glasses and perfect teeth,
and the way your head cocked to one side
when I asked a question.

Ed Malone was Randy's friend
Brylcreem crew-cut wave and freckles
and dazzling diamond eyes with long, long lashes.
We'd go back to your mini-Cape in Kingston
after school but I don't remember what we did.
What were those quiet afternoons for, Ed?
How did we star students pass the time:
playing chess, or Scrabble, maybe?
We were too grown-up to play doctor
the way I did it in Bobby Sherman's hayloft.
What did we talk about?
Sometimes my parents took us
to your father's big-booth
seafood emporium on Plymouth Harbor,
but you weren't there, of course,
the young prince of the place.

I loved to stare into your eyes,
although I didn't know it.
A fanboy wonder about—what?
The girls adored you—Linda, Judy, Terrell—
but you weren't into them.
You were the novice,
eyes on another, greater prize:
insurance.

I went away to school and left you all.
Randy and Donnie stayed put; now they're gone.
I was sweet on them. I had a chthonic crush

on moccasined Todd Mendham.
But, Ed, you were the dreamboat—
the drowning eyes, the spittled lips,
my Andy before Andy,
another one who got away.

Life is full-time in Oyster Ponds.
The garden's tired, the annuals
are blowsy, stems are gray.
Lawns are shaggy, too dry to be mowed.
But still they haven't raised the nets
the way they did when Dr. No was here.
Are they going to give the vineyard up?

Life is life-size here in Hypoluxo
with its homely interests and tensions
and lulls and relaxations. Will Walt
get the variance to build his house
in back of Tina? (*Yes, he will.*)
Will the Lagioias be allowed
to tear down the old cottage
at the end of Captain's Way
and put up a McMansion, the way others have?
(*They won't; but Sandy Ephron
will restore it beautifully.*)
Someday will someone say
after we're long gone:
We live in the Esparza house?
Will the past go rancid in formaldehyde
and bury the present?
What do the citizens of Oyster Ponds
want these stunted trees to shade,

ghosts of the elms that canopied the streets
like the noble ones I grew up under,
before Dutch elm disease
decimated every village green in the East?
(Does *decimate* mean reduce *by* ten percent
or *to* it?) Who decides
if Manny can serve dumplings
to incomers on Village Lane?
Who decides whose history this is,
and who it's for? Whose is this
pretend peace, perfect almost as peace?
Whose bones, if anyone's, are buried
in what was known as the slave graveyard?
The Historical Society
announced that they're determined to get at
"the truth" of the old Burial Ground
after someone got rid of the sign
that extolled the masters who had chosen
to rest forever with their "former servants"
(what did *they* choose?).
Darryl called it a fake
when he first saw it:
the stones too neat, too uniformly ranged,
with quahog shells adorning every grave,
the idyllic plot enclosed by old stone walls
chased with brambles, and the Bay beyond.
What is Oyster Ponds' true history?
A hundred years ago the Ku Klux Klan (who were they?)
would meet in the town hall
to terrify the Portuguese
who couldn't live on lower Village Lane.
(Workers from the Azores
harvested the bogs in Plympton every fall,
shadows on the landscape.

Where did they go
after the cranberries got raked
and the weather turned raw?)
Who's buried in the Burial Ground, if anyone?
Who's underneath the vineyard?
Who's in the Sampson cemetery
(they had the only documented slaves)?
Some claim the schoolhouse
was a barracks at the Point.
Dave remembers shacks in the back yard here
where people lived in summer
and cooked him dinner.
Infrared photography
shows there's no one buried in the graveyard.
But because there's nothing now
doesn't mean there wasn't something:
something that got moved, destroyed, decayed.
Water buries land,
land covers rock that came across the Sound
to pulverize whatever was here once.
The past is what the present says it was
till someone takes the sign away
or moves the pretty stones and says,
It was like this.
Oyster Ponds was farms
and someone did the planting,
the weeding and the winnowing.
Someone does it now, against the sun
in the dahlia fields out toward the Point.
We're mapped onto each other, wed,
invested in knowing and not knowing,
and the shame of owning
who owes what to whom,
and what makes up—what does?—for cruelty.

Have you seen lady's slippers here,
the grail-flower of our childhood
in the sand pit in the woods behind the house,
unpickable endangered veined pink
testicle on a stem,
and the army of asparagus
that rose up overnight
in the field beyond the outhouse?
Bayberry funk on the hillside,
everyday burden, daily box of wood
to feed the kitchen stove,
faded orchard, soft-shoulder stone walls,
myrtle under the elm that had to come down,
hawthorn linden peony plum thicket:
someone's garden once.
Meanwhile the locusts hula here.
The vineyard waves in the morning breeze
and they're raising the nets at last.
It's the end of August.
The world coughs, awaiting resolution,
the afflatus rises with the tide
and the grape leaves gleam
in the uncovered sun. It's dry
but the grass is green again.
The water's cool. Hangdog hydrangeas,
salt-burn-frazzled goldenrod,
death's-head verbascum/mullein.
The field will come back
but it's gone for now.
Burnished days, gold early pre-fall elegy.
The rosehips perk up on the finished bushes,
but the trumpet vine's still fine
and the juniper and rhododendron
and Japanese black pine are used to it.

The sun rises over Loring's,
too far back for an easy look
and too far right above the breakers,
so we don't see it.
We see the disk, the breakers,
the storm surge on the rocks that will wear them down
in a mere hundred thousand years.
The beach just disappeared after Irene,
all but the boulders and the undersand,
the gray, cold, only-recent stone,
but it's here and the supertankers and ketches
and ferries in both directions
on the roller against
the gray-blue almost aquamarine—
not that blue, *this* one.

THE GOLDEN YEARS

Are these the golden years I keep on saying
I'm spending at the Landing
and you keep asking, When?
A gentle sunset slowly deliquescing,
glinting across the course and into the woods
and over the Sound as day cools
and traffic rolls by the Iconic Snack Bar
and the Ninth Hole (closed now) that we always
said we should try.

The golden years—are these the ones
relieved of troubles, stoppered loves,
and climate amendments,
just meek acceptance and a decent dinner,

and TV until fade-out,
traffic whooshing off the ferry
on its way to Riverhead or somewhere
with its chores and ambitions

while we sit here enjoying?
It's all good, Dave assures us, yes and no,
fade-out like this ever-loving sunset
inching toward the Sound and heading westward
until you hit the Continental Shelf.

The premixed margaritas at the Lighthouse
are truly terrible—why did we have them?
Because you want to sample everything
the same way Louie needs
to visit every drawer every day:
every sandwich shop on University Place,
which is fun the way things are
in the golden years.

Is this it, the sunset stealing
over the evening grass
so soft, so gold, so orange,
slowly creeping toward the Sound and then the Shelf
so stealthily that I won't even notice
when you shut my eyes?

I wanted Montauk daisies as a hedge
against the hard days when the light
gets crabbed and sharp,
to help with the calm by the corrugated ponds
and Hokusai's wind-racked cherry
bending over the back bay,

its paper flowers as thick as cherry blossoms,
and the high-tide bushes we ignored all summer
in full bloom now on the causeway
and everywhere on Narrow River
and the afternoon stop-time when we say,
in spite of everything,
in spite of the wreckage, we knew it when we saw it:
is a little temporary permanence
too much to ask?
Dave and Walt spent Sunday fishing
trash out of the Sound.
The floor is strewn with it.
People are tossing garbage
off their boats as you read this.
I can taste it in the water.
Don't you feel it gnawing at the causeway
with our jellyfish cousins
and the beads of plastic in your brain
while we nibble our handhelds?

And the fawn is gone
that skittered across the lawn one afternoon
short-eared to our surprise
to fold her pins and wait trembling by the trash cans
for her mother out carousing,
or maybe just feeding.
After two nights she was gone,
no sign of mayhem, no red paint on the grass.
She came by night. They come by night
and nibble the hydrangeas
and hollyhocks and lilies, the fuckers,
here on our threshing floor,
and the squirrels keep laying up
provisions for when?

Remember sugar sandwiches? Remember restaurants?
We're coming back
but what we're coming back to
is something that was never here before.
Or else we're moving into the headwind
of a future more vivid before we fold,
what we were going to pass on
slipping from our hands.
All we do is shuffle stuff around
the young could not care less about.
Someday they'll wake up and hanker after
the silver and chairs and contentions
we had no one to pass on to.
And it will be too late.
But, Tityrus, let's do it anyway,
let's take the ride up Village Lane,
your long legs bowing on your too-short bike,
your red cap almost cutting off the view,
past the mailbox
with its shameful Confederate flag
and the glacial boulders—someone's dolmens?—
that are what we're given to know of the Pleistocene,
past the hallowed spot where you split your lip
and grew the beard that's so much grayer now.
Roll down the hill between the locusts
to the Sound that's free of jellyfish
now another August is behind us,
the Sound that's like an ocean without sound,
heavy shallow heaving like the world asleep,
and the power plant in the distance
and black-sailed boats like Theseus at Sounion
and the motorboat wake and my little dream house
over the bracken pond and carpenter bees
eating the porch and the everyday

loss of Eurydice in the new border
we're here just long enough to futz with
—not for trees (but you are).
The windows are open,
and the air has the run of the house.
New leaves emerge on the vines
as spring scrawls its name on the slate.
Already there are new notes on the staves
and the mulberry bursts into lime-green flame.
Shuffle and click and the staves get filled.
The orchestra's in tune and the new vines climb.
Pretend peace breaks out.
The sea of sea asparagus
will wax red like coral in the marsh.
The turkey families
will come from the tree farm
to winnow the grapes,
one coven waiting politely
or is it prudently to take its turn.
The ponds are mirrors,
the purple tufts of cane, the crickets,
the blotched blades of zebra grass,
the hibiscus preen, the insects skim the surface,
and the red ivy stole into the hedge.
It's forty-six degrees October 31st
and the leaves of the crape myrtle
are finally on fire now that we're leaving.
What will the old root do next year,
and Freddie's irises?
How will the new crape myrtles fare—
did they survive the young bucks' rack attacks
and winter's grab bag of indignities?
And the view from the Painter's window
with the old boat in its blue—

no, stainless gray—tarpaulin?
If there were just a fireplace,
I could sit and listen to you practice.
We'd bend to our phones and bask in summer's glories,
remember and anticipate the vineyard,
gold-green carpet at the height of summer,
bodacious banner, music being written.
Even if it didn't come again,
even if we won't be back, we'll know
the vineyard was here.

*

Eclogue

for Mark

The cottonwoods shoulder the river through the valley
as it ambles out of the Crazies sauntering
before it joins up with the Musselshell
and makes a fuss, the way desire
can well up before it settles into dailiness.
Somewhere near Two Dot it feathers in
to the fretwork of the longest river,
American Fork water, Yellowstone water,
winking and waving as it passes Biloxi
to marry the Gulf.
That's how you know it's there
when you scan the land: an emerald ribbon
snaking through the bush,
like the Clark Fork of the Yellowstone
two hundred miles away,
which is nothing.

Our second day you took us for a hike,
bear spray strapped to your belt, though what we saw
were the omnipresent deer, whitetail and mule,
and the sandhill cranes, in pairs as always,
with their tin-can rattle, claiming the fields.
Later, where the beaver ponds create
a marshy meadow we got eyed by my first moose,
baleful at two hundred yards,
before he got bored and moved on.

There are a lot of Crazies here—
Crazy Mountains, Crazy Canyons, Rivers,

crazy women who lost someone
and holed up alone, the stories say.
This primeval world is all curated:
if you look west and south
you don't see the wind farms,
or the missile silo on the ridge.
On Corbin Butte,
the Crow had lookouts where the cairns are,
or else the herders built them to survey
their flocks across the distance.
On my iPhone what you see
is a broad foreground that demands correction,
and low hills fading to a curved horizon,
the converse of the real height and hugeness.
That's what the lens does, says Tityrus:
it helps until it doesn't. The buffalo, you call them,
shaped this all a thousand years ago,
before the ruminating sheep tugged out the grass
and the club moss crept in.
That's why you need the acreage:
the cattle graze the way the bison did,
rolling, maddened by the flies,
pushing up the humps that had to be leveled.

To the eye that organizes everything,
pastoral is history.
In the big house are fauna on the mantel:
cougar, bison, elk; the Crow
that Joe De Yong's scenes heroize;
lassoing, branding,
the horses' shrunken withers
and clenched butts huddled in the weather.
It's a temple to the inland sea,
the dinosaurs, the Indians, the Rough Rider,

the New Yorkers' sapphire water goblets.
Now it's our time to imbibe the quiet
and give the will a free ride for a while.
Here in late June it's still spring,
the peonies are fisted,
waiting to unfurl their petticoats
like hussies in the brick hotels
that advertise Gold Rush mythologies.
There are no shadows in haunted Harlow,
only the pawnshop city hall
bunted and beribboned for the holiday.
The semis pushing through can't touch the pastness.
And we were too busy driving north
to stop for fireworks and blow stuff up.

It's not quite true that everything we see
is yours. Porcupine Butte
lowers across the valley, there's the Drews,
the Macks whose grasslands run up to the mountains,
the Fielding Ranches and egregious Andrew,
and your friend who owns Horse Butte.
We missed the calving but we saw the baler
lay an enormous egg in the upper field.
One afternoon the jeep sank in a ditch;
Joe and Ed had to drag it out with a pickup.
Slaphappy, we struggled home thigh-deep in mud,
soaked to our skins under the frizzing rainbows.

The next morning the heifer and the donkey
were waiting by the cabin door again.
Tityrus made pancakes. Thanks and embraces,
then up the long rise through the sheep gate,
down the buffalo jump canyon,
past the Melville church swamped by alfalfa,

the Crazies ratifying everything.
Then up and over the ice-cream Cascades
who haven't heard yet that the cake is melting,
and lakelocked Seattle, another native place
looking safe in spite of our best efforts.
No doubt we'll be reoriented soon,
but I'm far less sure that we'll recover.

*

Orient Epithalamion

For Barry Bergdoll and Bill Ryall

Fall will touch down in golden Orient,
where ospreys float and peace comes dropping slow.
There will be pumpkins by the ton at Latham's.
The trees will re-rehearse their yearly show.

But now crape myrtle ornaments the village,
rose of Sharon, autumn clematis.
The oyster ponds are dark and tranquil mirrors
basking in the sunlight's brazen kiss.

On Skipper's Lane, Sebastian and Sarah
have packed up with their brood, as one expects,
and Madeline and Chris, and Jane and Eddie.
No more artists! No more architects!

just Miriam and Grayson, Sylvia and Freddie.
Gone: writers, artists, publishers, and all!
The real people, proudly holding steady,
will reap the blond munificence of fall.

Farewell to the disturbances of summer,
when Stevie's singers jazzed in Poquatuck
and a Supreme Court Justice read our rights out
to every citizen, man, doe, and buck.

Now egrets dot the marsh on Narrow River.
The swan is hiding till she nests next spring.
Virginia creeper reddens on the tree trunks
and goldenrod envelops everything,

succeeding to swamp rose and honeysuckle
and all the weeds that came and went in waves.
The geese will soon be flying in formation
where the Tuthill slaves sleep in their graves.

Near the monarch station, the Holzapfels
harvest their garlic. Milkweed is in flower.
Leslie's pool is cooling down. The ferry
disgorges only fifty cars an hour.

It's time for sweet bay scallops, now the jellies
have turned tail in the Sound and run away.
The Bogdens check their conch pots every morning,
and the water climbs in Hallock's Bay.

Charles the First is staking lilies. Sinan
reduces his last oozings, hours by hours.
Karen surveys the still street from her study.
Charles the Second's arms are full of flowers.

And the turkeys make their first appearance,
as bay and sound still glisten from the Hill.
The vineyard grapes hang blithe and ripe and ready.
Ann builds her house, and Barry marries Bill.

Wreathe them with sea lavender and asters!
Sing for the joys and years they have in store.
Husband them; preserve them from disasters.
Let there be jazzing in the deep heart's core—

and let the tide not overwhelm the causeway.
May Orient be theirs forever more!

A NOTE ABOUT THE AUTHOR

Jonathan Galassi is the author of three previous poetry collections and two novels, and has published translations of the Italian poets Eugenio Montale, Giacomo Leopardi, and Primo Levi. A lifelong denizen of book publishing, he lives in New York City.

A NOTE ON THE TYPE

The text in this book was set in Miller, a transitional-style typeface designed by Matthew Carter (b. 1937) with assistance from Tobias Frere-Jones and Cyrus Highsmith of the Font Bureau. Modeled on the roman family of fonts popularized by Scottish type foundries in the nineteenth century, Miller is named for William Miller, founder of the Miller & Richard foundry of Edinburgh. The Miller family of fonts has a large number of variants for use as text and display, as well as Greek characters based on the renowned handwriting of British classicist Richard Porson.

Composed by North Market Street Graphics
Lancaster, Pennsylvania

Book design by Pei Loi Koay